WHAT WE LEAVE

WHAT WE LEAVE

Collected Poems

Benjamin Daniel Lukey

To Megan

TABLE OF CONTENTS

I

THE GREATEST OF THESE

The talking heads will babble
And weigh you down with trouble
And fill you with dismay,
But do not heed the pundits
For trouble has its limits
And Love can win the day.

For Love, dear friend, is stronger
Than hatred, greed, or anger,
And more to be revered
Than wisdom, wealth, or courage—
Than power, strength, or knowledge—
And never to be feared.

It won't be comprehended;
It cannot be demanded,
Yet it is free to all.
It wears the oldest mantle,
And though its mien is gentle,
Its subjects are in thrall.

For Love is God's own essence!
To Love we owe obeisance,
And how can we refuse?
So be you saint or sinner,
Take up Love's splendid banner
And go and spread the news.

Go forth and love your neighbors!
Go fan the dormant embers!
It has been said before:
That Love, dear friend, is stronger
Than prejudice or anger
And Love must win the war.

An Understatement

Tonight: me and you,

On the lake, in a canoe.

Oh, yes—that would do.

BELOVED

To know you is to love you.
What a blessing it is
That you are mine!
While I breathe, I am yours.

To know you is to love you.
I know you better than anyone,
And so I love you in equal measure.
I'll love you still more, someday.

Every day I see more clearly
What a blessing it is
That my soul is bound to yours
With links forged in Heaven.

Not a day goes by
That I don't thank God
That you are mine
To have and to hold.

I don't know where life will lead,
But I know who will go with me.
Whatever else may happen,
While I breathe, I am yours.

PARTNERS IN CRIME

I come

To you today

With yet another scheme

For a wild, foolish adventure.

Coming?

GONE FISHING

I've come to find that I am not my own.
There was a time this might have baffled me,
But not so now that I am fully grown.

I've said, "With me is where you ought to be."
If I can make that claim, then so can you;
To love is to possess, to some degree.

And if that's so, then this is also true:
The time I count my own is yours, in part—
And I cannot begrudge what love is due.

But I thank God it doesn't break your heart
That there are times I need to be alone.
Our love does not abate when we're apart.

Our love, my dear, is like a precious stone:
More equal to the years than flesh and bone.

LOOM

The warp and the weft

Of our hearts, minds, and spirits

Move in different ways,

But never separate.

The Lord weaves them together.

SOUVENIRS

Washing dishes
And folding sheets
Can make you feel so empty.

You had looked forward
To this visit
For so long.

You know what they say:
Anticipation is sweeter
Than what you anticipate.

What you dreamed of for months
Happened in days, and ended
As quickly as a goodbye.

But is it really gone—
And is anticipation
More substantial than memory?

Every smile, laugh, and embrace
Is surely more real now
Than when you looked forward to it.

HONOR

Love is the castle

He would defend with his life,

And love is the sword

He will fall upon someday.

UNSOLICITED ADVICE

I
Would like
To tell you
That everything
Will come out all right,
But would you believe me?
How can you, who think much, be
Anything but apprehensive?
How hard it is to live forwards, when
Life can only be understood backwards!

I do not try to understand my life.
I could never step back far enough
To see the whole picture at once.
I must take it as it comes,
Give thanks, and do my best.
Why should we worry?
What will it solve?
For better
Or worse,
Live.

A ROUNDED STONE

He pressed a rounded stone into my hand.
He said, "Take care of this," and turned away
To tend to things we needed for our trip:
The boats, the lines, the paddles, and the rest.

The stone was not like those about my feet.
I wondered at the stone, but not for long.
I put it in my pocket and forgot.

The Huzzah winds along a valley floor
Between thick stands of trees and rocky bluffs.
Its water is a marvel to behold,
Like crystal ichor flowing in God's veins.
I thought of all these things, and not the stone,
But in my pocket it was safe and sound.

And that was well, for when we came ashore
My uncle asked me for the rounded stone.
He placed it on the bank beside its twin.

"As easy as it was for you," he said,
"To bring this back to where I picked it up,
So light you sit within your Maker's hand.
The stone was not aware you carried it,
And sometimes we are just the same. But He
Is wise, and kind, and big and strong enough
To bring you safely to your journey's end.
We're going where we came from." So he said.

I miss him, but I know we'll meet again.

II

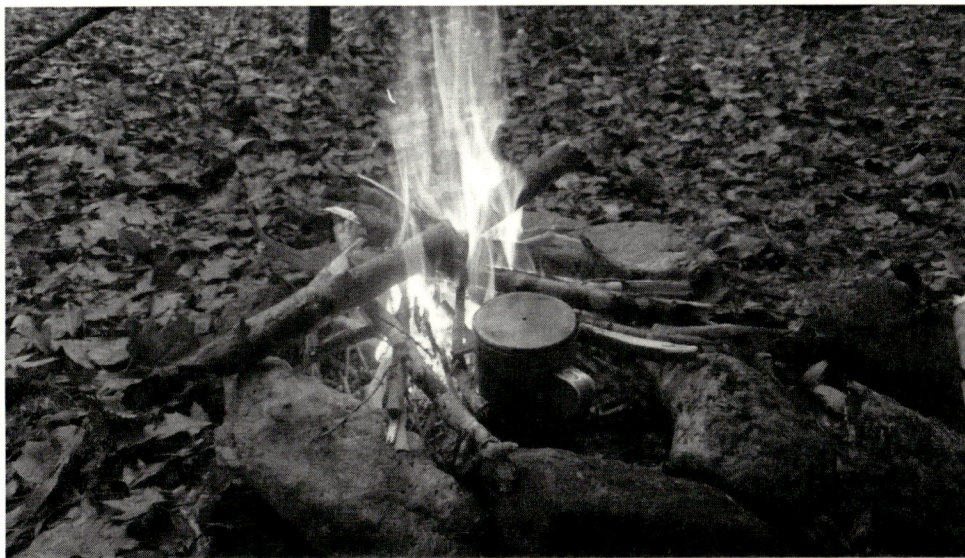

HUNGER

Silent and stately,

The prince of the great forest

Comes to feed in his meadow.

The hunter gives thanks.

Providence has smiled on him:

Here is food for his children.

THE SLEEP OF WOODSMEN

When evening finds me on some wooded rise,

Or else the level ground along a stream,

A heaviness descends upon my eyes

And Nature takes the semblance of a dream.

For I have known a peace beyond repose,

In rest unlike the comfort of a bed.

Though some men's brows are furrowed while they doze,

The woodsman's sleep is like that of the dead.

Go find a spot beneath the open sky,

And drape the night like blankets 'round your form!

The ground will be the couch where you will lie;

Though it be cold, the campfire-hearth is warm.

Recline at ease in Mother Nature's arms,

And be surrendered to her Morphean charms.

A BLUE BLAZE

Upon this ancient hickory, there is a blaze of blue.

To guess the meaning of this paint is more than I can do.

It does not seem to mark a trail; there are no other signs,

And blue is not the proper hue to mark one's boundary lines.

What errand was the painter on? Who made this mark, and why?

And who can follow where he led?

Can anyone?

Can I?

LOOK

A well-worn game trail,
Long used by deer and rabbits,
Has been rudely blocked

By an old cedar.
Time and disease wasted it,
And its roots gave way.

See, here, what is left
Of its long, feathered branches:
Spikes, long as my hand!

The deer do not mind,
For their legs are long enough
To step over it.

But the poor rabbits—
See by their tracks, here, and here—
Must all turn aside.

For it is too tall
To safely leap over it.
Look: one of them tried.

His blood stains this branch,
Dry, but still brilliant crimson,
In a wreath of fur.

What was chasing him?
He thought, on the open trail,
He could outrun it.

Perhaps he could have,
Were it not for this blockade.
What a wicked end!

And just to this side
The trunk is bare of branches.
He could have made it.

He missed by inches
And paid for it with his life.
Look before you leap.

THE BROOK

With a quiet voice,

The brook sings for anyone

Who cares to listen.

I have heard this song before,

But I'll never tire of it.

AND THESE THY GIFTS

Breakfast for dinner:

A bright smear of marmalade

On a toasted sky.

RECURRENT

This rain fell before,

Somewhere. Soon, it will ascend

To fall somewhere else.

THE RIVER

The river does not care whether I live or die.

In the spring, he swells with the rain and flows swiftly
And tears mercilessly at the earth, as though in pursuit of some hidden foe.
Men say at such times that he is angry, but it is not wrath that drives him.
He is full and fat and drunk with springtime,
And mad as the hares in the meadows above his banks,
But not angry.

He is without malice and without compassion.

Late in the year he flows slowly—calmly, some say—
But the gentleness with which he bears my boat downstream
Is the same as the gentleness with which he touches all things.
Gently he bears a leaf, a twig, an empty bottle
Cast aside by some careless fisherman.
Gently he brushes away the soil of his banks
Until the mighty sycamores tumble in.
Gently he bears their pale bodies along
Until they become heavy with water
And sink to corruption in his insatiable belly.
And with immense, unceasing, indifferent gentleness,
He slides over the face of the earth,
Turning stone to gravel to sand to nothing.

The river does not care whether I live or die.

I know him better than friend or blood.
I know the shallow, sun-mottled places where deer come to drink of him.
I know the deep and dark places where fat old fish swim lazily,
Half-asleep and out of the sun's reach.
I know the quiet places where ducks and geese come to rest
And the great blue heron stands motionless as a statue
Carved in the likeness of some ancient pagan sky-god.

I know where ripples on the river's surface
Warn of his jagged rock-teeth just below.
I know where his rapids and falls
Hide
Out of sight
Around the bend
Ready to wreck the boats
And break the bodies of careless men.

The river does not care whether I live or die.

He speaks, and I know his language.
He tells stories to anyone who knows how to listen—
Tales of ages gone by and countless seasons of plenty and drought.
I read the tracks in his walls and see what his shape once was,
And guess at what it will be a thousand years after I am gone.
His fierce beauty haunts my dreams
And fills me with discontentment for the work I must do
Before I can paddle and fish and swim again.

The river calls me, and I will answer.

But first, I will send a prayer to Him who made the river.
I will thank Him for His wondrous creation
And for the time I have been given on this world.
I will ask Him for fair weather and safe passage,

Because the river does not care whether I live or die.

ANTICIPATION

Since dawn

I've been sitting

In this boat, eagerly

Longing for the line's twitch that says

"Breakfast!"

HUNTING

I call my cat's name.

The response: a plaintive shriek!

She has a field mouse.

"Well done," I say, and wonder

If anyone will miss him.

CONSTELLATION

You see a pendant

Hanging from a silver chain.

I see faithful hounds

Just ahead of the huntress:

Bright planets above the moon.

A TRICK OF THE EYE

Cold, unearthly light:

A herd of deer is grazing

(It seems) on the moon.

TO A DEER

By what right do I take your life today?
Your flesh and blood are not unlike my own.
The same Hand made us both, and gave to you
More grace of form and motion than to me.
It is by reason of that grace you live
Not only in the forests of this world,
But also in the hearts and minds of men—
In history, in legend, and in song.

Your name was often on King David's lips—
But then again, he sang of hunters too.
And many generations earlier,
God said to Noah that all moving things
Were food for man—and after David's time,
He spoke to Peter, saying, "kill, and eat!"

By what right does the wolf feed on your kind?
By what right does the cat devour the bird?
To live is to be hungry, and if you
Had fangs and claws, you would not feed on grass.

If honor is a thing that you can know,

I hope that you will see some honor in

The great pains I must take to bring you down.

There is no wrath or greed in what I do.

We must all die someday, and I will strive

To make this death the best one you could have—

And you, as all your ancestors have done,

Will live on in the hearts and minds of men.

Your life will nourish mine, and I will try,

As I have always done, to live a life

Deserving of what God has given me.

And now, farewell—I send you to your rest.

UNANSWERED

Questions in the wind—

It sounds like the owl says *who*,

But it might be "Why?"

TRUDGE

In a field of wheat,

A slow ripple shows me where

Some unseen creature

Is pushing stubbornly through

With who-knows-how-far to go.

WANDERER

Look back and try to understand
The winding roads by which you came.
If you are lost, who is to blame?
You've traveled far—at whose command?

You've wandered from the way you planned
To parts where no one knows your name.
Look back, and try to understand
The winding roads by which you came.

At journey's end, where will you stand?
The young are wild; the wise grow tame.
In seeking help there is no shame.
Will you refuse a guiding hand?
Look back, and try to understand.

BOY

I used to know a little boy.

I used to be him.

Lately, I've been looking at my life

And wondering what he would think of it.

We still talk from time to time,

But with every conversation we seem to know each other less.

Nothing I say makes sense to him.

Everything he says is in the future tense:

Places he will go, people he will meet,

Amazing things he will do.

He cannot understand my past-tense explanation

That I never got around to doing those things.

I cannot bear the look of reproach he gives me.

He doesn't understand.

He wants impossible things!

I wanted impossible, childish things. I still do.

...but when I became a man, I put away childish things.

Maybe I shouldn't have put all of them away.

Maybe I didn't.

Now and then, I come across one where I least expect to find it:

When I read a ghost story or a book about pirates,

When I sip a mug of hot cocoa,

When I ride my bicycle—

When I float down a river,

Set a trotline, make shelter for the night,

Cook supper over a fire—

Every time I make a new friend,

Every time I go someplace I've never been before,

Every time I learn something new

And take a moment to marvel at it—

Every time my imagination transforms a woodlot into a wilderness

Or an inconvenience into an adventure,

I smile a childish smile

As my hopeful past touches a present that seems impossible

And reaches for a future that no longer does.

I am a little boy,

But I have done some amazing things,

And I will do more before I am through.

III

AN OLD ROADBED

This was a road; an old map told me so.

A trail, I'd say, and sometimes less than that.

It's hard to walk, and harder still to know.

It started as an even bed of chat.

A mile beyond the gate, it turned to clay,

And here the leaves have not been trampled flat.

I look between the trees to guess my way:

Among the oaks, a space one wagon wide.

Who drove here? Are their sons alive today?

And can I rightly say the old map lied?

The future's not what maps are made to show.

Life's like this road—it cannot be denied:

The way's less clear the further in you go.

It's hard to walk, and harder still to know.

BUGBEAR

The bee means no harm.

Show neither fear nor anger,

And all will be well.

THE CALLING

The Calling comes at different times to each,
And will be heard by eager souls who yearn
For something great to be, or do, or learn.
My Calling, when I heard it, was to teach.
What lofty heights of knowledge one might reach!
For questions, kindled, can forever burn
And light the way for thought, which may, in turn,
Give birth to noble action and fair speech.

But if I fail, my students also fall!
And so my constant fear is that I may
Confound my pupils with my rambling words.
To those placed in my care I'll give my all.
God grant that I might have the words to say!
God help me to protect these fledgling birds.

WONDER

For Marc Pooler

Heaven seems smaller
To learned astronomers
Than it does to wide-eyed babes.

They are blessed who find
A wide-eyed astronomer
To teach their children wonder.

FRIENDSHIP

What is friendship for,
But to help you see the world
In ever-new ways?
My best friend already knows
The next thing I need to learn.

THE CLOCKMAKER

When I was young, I'd disassemble clocks
So I could understand what made them go.
With tools in hand, and pieces in a box,
I'd wonder, and I'd look, and then I'd know.
But lacking tools to take *myself* apart,
I understand myself through what I'm told,
And one friend told me I am young at heart—
Another said my soul is very old.
If I can trust them both (I think I can),
Then I have been—*repaired*, or else restored.
Is it sometimes the lot of broken man
To go back to the workshop of the Lord?
Some say that Great Clockmaker stands aloof,
But I know otherwise—and I'm the proof!

OUT OF FUTILITY, UTILITY

Don't try to write with a dull pencil.

Do some *constructive destruction*

(thoughtful, deliberate waste).

Strip away all that's dull

to make a sharp point.

You're left with less

but sometimes

"less" is

more

.

How I Got This Way

Uneasy in the company of friends,

I felt no better sitting by myself;

Improving means had not improved the ends.

So I took *Walden* from my bedside shelf,

And on page nine, I nodded off at last—

And dreaming, met the spirit of Thoreau.

The specter spread his arms and cried,

                          "Avast!

Oh, why so seeming fast but deadly slow?

You lead a life of quiet desperation—

But if you look about you, you will find

Pasture enough for your imagination!

Go out, and try to hear what's in the wind!"

So I awoke, wrapped in a reverie,

And went to seek the things I could not see.

HARDSHIP AND DESTINY

Weddington High School, Matthews, North Carolina
Graduation Day, June 2, 2021

A wise man once said, "Hardships often prepare ordinary people for extraordinary destiny." His name was C.S. Lewis, and as far as I can tell, he usually knew what he was talking about. And maybe that's the silver lining in this weird, cloudy time we've been living in. We have all faced some hardships lately, and we can hope that the healing and growing you've done in response to those hardships have prepared some of you for extraordinary destiny.

I tried hard to remember what I needed to hear when I was sitting in your seat. That was a long time ago—it was almost exactly half of my lifetime—but I think I remember needing advice from people who weren't my parents. I hadn't yet learned the value of listening to them; I didn't learn that until I was about twenty-two, and I really hope it doesn't take you that long.

I want to tell you about some things that I believe everyone needs in order to succeed. I won't need to say much about the first two, because you already have them. Every one of you. They are *optimism* and *curiosity*. A wise woman once said, "Optimism is the faith that leads to achievement. Nothing can be done without hope and confidence." Her name was Helen Keller. A man famous for his knowledge and wisdom once said that he had no special talent—that he was only "...passionately *curious*." His name was Albert Einstein. If you don't know why I think it's important to heed Keller's words about optimism or Einstein's words about curiosity, there are some books you should read. And if you ask me, I'll help you find them. But back to that claim I made a moment ago: that every one of you has cultivated the virtues of optimism and curiosity. I won't pretend that you all have them in equal measure, but you couldn't have gotten to where you are without them. And if you reflect on your education, you'll realize that the moments when you demonstrated the most optimism and curiosity were the

44

moments when learning was easiest, most meaningful, and most fun. Please don't forget that.

Looking ahead, I can't tell you everything you'll need to know, because I've only been given four hours to speak. *Tee hee hee.* Looking ahead, I can't tell you everything you need to know because you'll all need to know different things. Each of you will need different knowledge, skills, and virtues to succeed in your chosen fields. Some of you will be leaders, and some of you will be followers, and that's okay. A wise man once said, "Whatever you are, be a good one." His name was Abraham Lincoln. I can't tell you how to be a good lawyer, doctor, senator, electrician, soldier, dog groomer, or pastry chef, but I can tell you three things that every single one of you will need to do in order to really succeed in life: be *patient*, be *kind*, and when you can help it, *don't* be *stupid*.

Let me explain that last one first. A wise man once said, "Life is tough, but it's tougher when you're stupid." His name was John Wayne. And if his words or my repetition of them offend you, there's a good chance that you and I mean different things when we say the word *stupid*. Most people your age, and some people my age, use it as an antonym of *intelligent*, but I don't think that's the right way to use it. I believe that *stupid* is what happens by default to every one of us when we stop thinking. It doesn't matter how intelligent you are; stupidity is, unfortunately, always an option. And if you don't believe me, ask the smartest people you know to tell you about the stupidest things they've done. Some of those stories will be really funny, but many of them will be heartbreaking. Make no mistake: stupidity lurks inside every single one of us, just waiting for moments of inattention when it can leap out and cause broken dishes, and spilled paint, and burned fingers, and bad grades—and traffic accidents—and broken relationships. As you go out into the world, shouldering more responsibility than ever before, you *can't stop thinking*, especially at moments when you hold your life or the lives of other people in your hands—like every single time you get behind the wheel of a car.

Even if you are exceptionally careful and attentive, and you manage to keep stupidity from knocking you off course, as you work toward your goals, you'll make a frustrating and sometimes painful discovery: everything in life that is worth doing will take longer than you want it to. I don't know why that is, but it's true. You can do everything just right, working as diligently and quickly as possible, but you will still spend much of your life *waiting*. And that's a bitter pill to swallow. A wise man once said, "Patience is bitter, but its fruit is sweet." His name was Aristotle. Perhaps the promise of an eventual reward for your patience seems insignificant compared to the awful feeling that your time is being wasted. To even the most patient person, too much waiting can feel hopeless. Patience can feel like a weakness, but a wise man once said, "Patience is not passive...it is concentrated strength." His name was Bruce Lee, and he knew about strength. If patience is something you struggle with, consider the words of a wise man who said, "The secret to patience is having something else to do in the meantime." His name was Croft Pentz. When it feels that your life has been interrupted, and you must wait, *do* things. Make things. Learn things. Keep a good book with you at all times, even if it's on your phone. If you need a book, let me know! I have lots of books. I'll give you one.

But when you find yourself needing to exercise patience, it's likely that the best thing you can do with your time is to look for opportunities to be kind to people. A wise man once said, "We cannot live only for ourselves; a thousand fibers connect us with our fellow men, and along those fibers...our actions run as causes, and return to us as effects." His name was Henry Melvil. It doesn't matter how independent you are; you will always be connected, in good or bad ways, with the people around you. No matter who you are, no matter how much money you make, the single most important thing you can do to improve your quality of life is to cultivate *positive* relationships through kindness. You can't ultimately control how everybody treats you, but you can control how you treat them, and that's what really matters—and people won't forget your kindness. A wise woman once said, "...people will forget what you said, people will forget what you did, but people will never forget how you made them feel." Her name was Maya Angelou. Mark Twain called kindness "...the language that the deaf can hear and the blind can see." And those words are not an empty exaggeration. He knew what he was talking about. He was almost certainly thinking of his deaf and blind friend Helen Keller when he said them.

Don't ever underestimate the value of being kind. It will nourish your soul, especially when it's difficult. You will meet people who are very hard to be kind to, but you should try to be kind to them anyway. And if you're ever unsure of *how* to be kind to those people, there's really only one thing you need to keep in mind, and it's very simple. It's not always easy, but it is always simple. To paraphrase the words of a very wise man: treat other people the way you want to be treated. It seems to me he knew what he was talking about.

Those of you who know me well won't be surprised to learn that I have composed a poem for this occasion. And unfortunately, because you have selected me to speak at this solemn and joyous occasion, now you have to listen to it—but it's not very long. It's only a sonnet. Fourteen lines and then I'll shut up.

> The time is now at hand; the bow is bent
> To shoot you forth across the open sky.
> And as you think on what these years have meant,
> You may know where you wish to land, and why.
> Or else you may believe you hold the bow;
> An arrow cannot aim itself for flight.
> You've chosen paths to take; I hope you know
> Their ends are far beyond our power of sight.
> Some days, the way before you will seem bleak;
> Pursuit of happiness is arduous.
> Persist—and you will find the joy you seek.
> Please don't forget to send some back to us.
> We'll miss you so much more than we can tell,
> But we are proud to bid you all farewell.

IV

ATTACHED

Behind the curtains

Of this material world,

Spiritual hands

Pull to and fro on our hearts.

We decide which strings will break.

VISITATION

An unfamiliar sound disturbed my sleep—
And as I drew the curtains from my brain,
I there beheld a sight to make one weep:
The orphaned thought of some forgotten pain.

I knew her cherub face, but though I tried,
I could not couple it with any name.
And when I bade her speak, she only cried;
I felt her grief, but knew not whence it came.

Then nameless woe gave way to formless Fear—

I said to it, "If God has banished you
Once from my mind, you are not welcome here.
In His name, leave me now!"

                           It turned and flew
On wings of unaccountable despair,
With horns protruding from its golden hair.

HERALD

In the eastern sky,

A solitary star shines,

Piercing the darkness

And preparing a cold world

For the warm light of the Sun.

I Cannot Tell

I cannot tell what there will be
Of good or ill this day for me—
And so, before I greet the day,
I'll go before the Lord and pray
With humble heart and bended knee.

How to address the Deity
Who bought my soul to set me free?
What are the words that I should say?
I cannot tell.

O blessed, mighty Trinity
Who made the earth and sky and sea,
Be near and help me, so I may
Not stumble, fall, or lose my way.
What lies ahead? The Lord can see!
I cannot tell.

ON LEAVING MY HOUSE

The fires are out; the lamps are snuffed.

The door is locked; I've done enough.

I give my house and all my pelf

To God Almighty, who Himself

Will keep it safe or let it go.

The future is not mine to know.

And as 'twas said by God's own Son,

"Lord, not my will, but Thine be done."

THIN PLACES

Dawn

Broke at

The crossroads,

And there I saw

Improbable things

In the fog—and ahead,

A distant line of mountains

I had never noticed before.

Ethereal and mysterious,

They stood at least a day's ride to the west.

I nearly forgot my business in town

And rode instead for those phantom hills.

I heard the call to adventure,

And I drew breath to answer—

But then, to my dismay,

The hills became clouds.

As the sun rose,

Earth resolved

Into

Sky.

TRUTH

One should wait to say

The really important things

Until the morning

And the first cup of coffee.

In espresso veritas.

THE OLD-FASHIONED WAY

Just like they used to,
When your daddy was a boy,
Do things the right way.

Let your yes be yes—
But if you make a promise,
Keep it with your life.

Don't be impudent.
Respect the gray-headed ones.
Help them cross the street.

Don't wait 'til things break.
Trust in God, but change your oil.
Sharpen your pen-knife.

Get out the whetstone.
Fix up that dull edge right now,
Else it might cut you.

Don't waste and don't want.
Disposable is shameful.
Refill the Zippo.

Keep your two dollars.
Brew your own coffee at home.
Grind the beans yourself.

Say grace, and then eat.
What we have is good enough—
More than we deserve.

WHAT THE QUALITY EAT

(NONE OF YOUR LOW-DOWN CORN-PONE)

"How do you make your cornbread?"

                            "Let me see:

A cup of cornmeal, and a cup of flour,

A teaspoonful of salt. I think that's right;

I know I have it written down somewhere."

"And how much sugar?"

                      "Sugar?! Goodness, no!

Please do not speak that awful word again.

What was I saying? Cornmeal, flour, and salt...

And baking powder! One whole tablespoon.

You whisk these all together in a bowl.

And in a larger bowl, you beat two eggs

And add whole milk: one and a quarter cups.

And as you beat them, grab the other bowl

And slowly add the dry things to the wet.

A round cast-iron skillet's what you need:

Nine inches (eight or ten would likely work).

You heat the skillet on the stove to melt

Some bacon fat that you had saved before.

Two tablespoons or so should do the trick.

You tilt the skillet so it's coated well,
Then pour the extra grease into the bowl.
You mix the batter while the skillet heats,
And when it's nice and hot, you pour it in.

Now, don't forget to heat the oven up.
I probably should've mentioned that before.
Four hundred twenty-five degrees, I think.
As soon as you have poured the batter in,
You slide the skillet in and shut the door.
At twenty minutes, check for golden-brown,
Or use a toothpick: it should come out clean."

FAMILIAR

I hear

All the old things

Calling with sweet voices.

I didn't think I missed them, but

I did.

PHANTOMS

Alone in the woods,

I rest and smoke my cob pipe—

But am I alone?

Wreaths of white smoke surround me;

The forest seems full of wraiths.

SHARPENING TIME

How good it is to have my knife with me
When there are packages to open up,
Or kindling to split, or lines to trim!

And yes, of course, if worse should come to worst,
My knife may be my last line of defense.
A blade is good to have in peace or war.

You may have heard that Jesus told his men
To sell their cloaks, if need be, and buy swords.
I like to think he'd like this knife of mine.

Unfortunately, wise old Solomon,
Outspoken as he was against *dull* blades,
Would not approve of this: the sorry state
That I've allowed the edge to fall into.
It's long past time to get the file and stones.

"As iron sharpens iron," so the file
Will strip away the steel and shape an edge
That's fit to cut a rope, but not to shave.
A half-hour with the stones will do the rest.

I pray to God that I will never need
To use this blade for anything but work,
But I will sleep a little better when
I know my knife is sharp enough for war.

THE MESSAGE BOARD

WE HAVE CASH TO BUY YOUR UGLY HOUSE if you will sell it.

Someone has a truck for sale, but don't know how to spell it.

Handy numbers you can call when time is of the essence,

Babysitting, frisbee golf, guitar and banjo lessons.

Pups and kittens, ducks and chickens, rabbits, goats, and horses:

Sacrifices offered up to economic forces.

Business cards for people trapped in dying occupations—

Quiet cries for help disguised as friendly affirmations.

ESTATE SALE

After Robert Frost

What is this venerable, hard-used tool? What is it for?

It lies inert, its days of usefulness over: gone with the thought,

The informed, actionable thought, of the father. The son doesn't know what he has,

But with a sad look, he says he will be happy to sell it to you: "For a—"

(Here he hesitates) "—two dollars." He also points out a handsome pair

Of gold-colored cufflinks. He doesn't know what they are made of.

You wish you could meet the father and go out with him on the *Dauntless*

("Boat For Sale") but spirit and thought have been borne away on angels' wings.

V

DIRGE

The mourning doves land
In my pasture to tell me
Summer is ending.

THE LOAN

This life we hold so dear is but a loan.

For good or ill, its balance must be spent,

For life is not a thing that we can own.

The wasting of our fragile flesh and bone

Is not within our power to prevent.

This life we hold so dear is but a loan—

But brevity of life, which some bemoan,

Should but lend urgency to what is lent,

For life is not a thing that we can own.

Remember what you planted—what has grown?

It comes of what you've *done*, not what you meant.

This life we hold so dear is but a loan—

You cannot reap what you have never sown!

Waste not another day! Turn and repent,

For life is not a thing that we can own.

Spend life on those you love, or die alone—

And wonder, at the end, where it all went!

This life we hold so dear is but a loan,

For life is not a thing that we can own.

WHO MOURNS FOR YOU?

An owl's broken wing

Waves from the side of the road

In silent farewell.

RAIN

The wipers can clear

The water from her windshield

But not from her eyes.

FRAILTY

She knows it is time.

Her soul is straining to fly.

She is too weak to hang on.

He prays for more time.

Her heart is a part of him.

He is too weak to let go.

ADIUVA ME, DOMINE

Today, I mean to walk with Thee,
But I am bent with woe and care.
Please lay Thy gracious hand on me,
And take this load I cannot bear.

APOLOGY TO AN OLD FRIEND

I swore I'd keep in touch with you—
I crossed my heart and hoped to die.
I meant it, so it was no lie,
But as you know, it wasn't true.

OUR LAST GOODBYE

The last time that I said goodbye to you,
I didn't know that it would be the last,
but something in your voice—I think you knew.

I'm sorry that these years went by so fast.
I always meant to visit you again.
Somehow, I let you slip into my past
and vanish from my future. How and when
did it become impossible for me
to get to you? That's neither now nor then.

In heaven, we'll be given eyes that see
no *here* or *there*. Our hearts and minds will know
nothing of time. It is a place to *be*,
with nowhere else that one could wish to go.

And there, someday, we'll say our last hello.

ACKNOWLEDGMENTS

Thanks to the Lord, for making me, blessing me, and keeping me.

Thanks to Megan, for loving me.

Thanks to my family, for bringing me up in the way that I should go. Thanks especially to Mark and Martha Lukey, who are my heroes, and who also happen to be my parents.

Thanks to my friends, for understanding me.

Thanks to my teachers, for giving me their best even when I didn't give them mine. Thanks especially to Scott Revis, who showed me where to look, but didn't tell me what to see.

Thanks to my students, for teaching me so much.

Thanks to the editors of *Edify Fiction, The Mystic Blue Review, The Society of Classical Poets, Sincerely Magazine, Gathering Storm Magazine, The Ibis Head Review, Torrid Literature Journal, The Wire's Dream Magazine, Adelaide Literary Magazine, 50 Haikus, The Road Not Taken,* and *The Chained Muse,* for putting my work where readers could find it.

Thank you for reading.

PUBLICATION CREDITS

"An Old Roadbed" was first published by *Edify Fiction*.

"On Leaving My House" was first published by *The Mystic Blue Review*.

"A Rounded Stone"
"Apology to an Old Friend"
"The Clockmaker"
"The Sleep of Woodsmen"
"The Loan"
"To a Deer"
and "Hardship and Destiny" were first published by *The Society of Classical Poets*.

"An Understatement" was first published by *Sincerely Magazine*.

"Partners in Crime" was first published by *Gathering Storm Magazine*.

"Estate Sale" was first published by *The Ibis Head Review*.

"The Old-Fashioned Way"
and "The Calling" were first published by *Torrid Literature Journal*.

"Anticipation"
and "Phantoms" were first published by *The Wire's Dream Magazine*.

"Familiar"
"Beloved"
"Look"
and "The Greatest of These" were first published by *Adelaide Literary Magazine*.

"Truth" was first published by *50 Haikus*.

"A Blue Blaze" was first published by *The Road Not Taken*.

"Gone Fishing"
"Sharpening Time"
"Wanderer"
"I Cannot Tell"
"How I Got This Way"
"Visitation"
"Adiuva Me, Domine"
and "Our Last Goodbye" were first published by *The Chained Muse*.

Made in United States
North Haven, CT
01 February 2025